Cost of Living

Cost of Living

Martyna Majok

THEATRE COMMUNICATIONS GROUP
NEW YORK
2018

Cost of Living is published by Theatre Communications Group, Inc.,
520 Eighth Avenue, 24th Floor, New York, NY 10018-4156

"Broken Vessels," *Broken Vessels: Essays*, by Andre Dubus; David R. Godine, Publisher; Boston, 1992 (reprint edition). "Dancing After Hours," *Dancing After Hours: Stories*, by Andre Dubus; Vintage Books, a division of Random House; New York, 1996.

The publication of *Cost of Living* by Martyna Majok, through TCG's Book Program, is made possible in part by the New York State Council on the Arts with the support of Governor Andrew Cuomo and the New York State Legislature.

Special thanks to the Vilcek Foundation for its generous support of this publication.

TCG books are exclusively distributed to the book trade by Consortium Book Sales and Distribution.

Library of Congress Cataloging-in-Publication Data
Library of Congress Control Numbers:
2018032187 (print) / 2018034800 (ebook)
ISBN 978-1-55936-597-0 (trade paper) / ISBN 978-1-55936-910-7 (ebook)
A catalog record for this book is available from the Library of Congress.

Cover, book design and composition by Lisa Govan
Cover photo by Todd Hido / Edge Reps
Author photo by Tess Mayer

First Edition, September 2018
Fifth Printing, August 2023

For Paweł Majok

And I believe I can do this in an ordinary kitchen with an ordinary woman and five eggs . . . She and I and the kitchen have become extraordinary: we are not simply eating; we are pausing in the march to perform an act together; we are in love; and the meal offered and received is a sacrament which says: I know you will die; I am sharing food with you; it is all I can do, and it is everything.

—ANDRE DUBUS, "BROKEN VESSELS"

There's something about taking the cart back instead of leaving it in the parking lot . . . Because somebody has to take them in . . . And if you know that, and you do it for that one guy, you do something else. You join the world . . . You move out of your isolation and become universal.

—ANDRE DUBUS, "DANCING AFTER HOURS"

Czemu tak się rozsypujemy? Człowiek to głupio skonstruowany.
[Why do we crumble like this? People are stupidly engineered.]

—PAWEŁ MAJOK

Cost of Living

Ani (Katy Sullivan) and Eddie (Wendell Pierce) in the Williamstown Theatre
Festival production. Photo: Daniel Rader.

PRODUCTION HISTORY

Cost of Living received its world premiere on June 29, 2016, at
the Williamstown Theatre Festival (Mandy Greenfield, Artistic
Director) in Williamstown, MA. It was directed by Jo Bonney;
the set design was by Wilson Chin, the costume design was by
Jessica Pabst, the lighting design was by Jeff Croiter, the sound
design was by Ben Truppin-Brown, original music was by Justine
Bowe, the movement direction was by Thomas Schall; the production stage manager was David H. Lurie. The cast was:

EDDIE	Wendell Pierce
ANI	Katy Sullivan
JESS	Rebecca Naomi Jones
JOHN	Gregg Mozgala

Cost of Living received its New York premiere on June 6, 2017, at
the Manhattan Theatre Club (Lynne Meadow, Artistic Director;
Barry Grove, Executive Producer) at New York City Center. It
was directed by Jo Bonney; the set design was by Wilson Chin,
the costume design was by Jessica Pabst, the lighting design was
by Jeff Croiter, original music and sound design were by Robert
Kaplowitz, the movement direction was by Thomas Schall; the
production stage manager was David H. Lurie. The cast was:

EDDIE	Victor Williams
ANI	Katy Sullivan
JESS	Jolly Abraham
JOHN	Gregg Mozgala

Folks

EDDIE, male, late forties
ANI, pronounced "Ah-nee," female, early forties
JESS, female, mid-twenties
JOHN, male, mid-twenties

Place

The urban East of America. New Jersey.
The near present.

The Prologue, Scenes Seven, Eight and Nine occur on the same Friday night in December, a week before Christmas. The rest of the play spans September through December.

Dialogistics

Slashes // indicate overlap.
Ellipses . . . are active silences.
[Square brackets] are words intended but unspoken.
(Non-italicized parenthesis) within dialogue are meant to be spoken.

A Note on John's Language

John has a speech pattern that manifests itself in a kind of halted way of speaking. This is due to the vocal tension of his cerebral palsy. The breaks and spacing in his lines are meant to simulate that halting rather than to indicate any sort of poetic recitation.

Some Notes on Performance

Self-pity has little currency in these characters' worlds. Humor, however, has much.

For the Jersey mouth, the word "fuckin" is often used as a comma, or as a vocalized pause, akin to the word "like." ["I can't like, decide, y'know." = "I can't fuckin, decide, y'know."] It's a word with extra purpose. It's not necessarily *just* a container for anger.

A Note on Casting

Please cast disabled actors in the roles of John and Ani.

Please assemble a cast that looks like North Jersey and its beautiful diversity. In the Prologue, Ani's full name can be Ania Łucja Skowrońska-Torres or Ani Luz Hernandez-Torres or Ani Li-Torres or Ānanda Singh-Torres, amongst many options. Ani's full name should be chosen to suit the actress playing her. Also, in the prologue, *Na zdrowie* can be replaced with *Salud* or صحتك فى: or 건배, etc., to suit the actress playing Ani. In Scene Eight, the phone call should be translated into a non-English language to suit the actress playing Jess.

Prologue

An empty space. An empty stage. That is, a bar in December.
Specifically, St. Mazie's bar in post-Bloomberg Williamsburg, Brooklyn.
One might call it a hipster bar.

A man. Eddie Torres. An unemployed truck driver. He looks out of place here.

Eddie Torres is a man who understands that self-pity and moping are privileges for people who, in their lives, have friends and family who unconditionally love them and will listen to their shit. Anything he tells you, he hopes will be entertaining or funny or interesting because he knows you're not obligated to stay and listen to him. When he slips into sadness, he bounces back fast. He would have made a great uncle.

He nurses a glass of seltzer.

EDDIE
The shit that happens is not to be understood.

That's from the Bible.

The shit that happens to you is Not To Be Understood.

So, see, this fucked me up a little when one day comes this call from Columbia Presbyterian. Is this Mister Torres? There's been a complication. I'm forty-nine and I've done nothin but love the fuck outta this woman for two decades and a year almost. Nothin. Who deserves that?

And a week from her birthday. Seven days.

We were gonna go to Maine. For her birthday.
See the trees.

I leave the lights on now, every room.
Smoke signal: I'm still here.

Holidays are hard.
Christmas next week—that's gonna be hard.

But listen to me holy shit the GLOOM. Get a drink. On me. Made a promise to myself. A penalty. I start talkin gloom, I get it in the WALLET. Lemme buy you a drink. What do you want? Order what you want, I'm payin. This place is my fuckin SWEAR jar.

Order what you want. Go ahead.

Me myself personally, I'm off it. That first day you wake up to find you are *not* in a pool of some kinda liquid, my friend? Vomit, say, or piss? That day? That day is a beautiful fuckin gift upon yer life, man. You are grateful for that day. And you are ready.

That day's the day it's all gonna change.

Signs are real.

This I know cuz I used to drive trucks. Cross-country. Loved it. Loved every aspect of the job. The scenery. Every aspect. The fuckin *scenery*. Utah? Jesus H, man. Utah's gorgeous and no one even knows!

But then I got popped for a DUI. In a car. Blocks from home.
Lost my CDL.
Shit's Creek.
So I got the memories. And some unemployment.

That life is good for people. I was thankful for every day they ain't invented yet the trucker-robots. That life is good. The road. Sky. The scenery.
Except the loneliness.
Except in the case of all the, y'know, loneliness.
This was what my wife was good for.
Not that this was the only thing.

But everyone what's married there's, y'know, the *fuuuuck* days.
Like, *fuuuuck* what did I do. What did I actually fuckin do here.
Cuz, y'know, you married a *person*. And a person's gonna be a person even if they're married.
That's a lesson. That's a lesson for yer LIFE right there.

But still I
I still

still loved her.

She would text me. On the road.
At night. In motels.
Which, alone, can be, can drum up certain feelings.
This is why there's Bibles in motels.

We're all of us, in motels, on the road to somewhere we ain't at
yet and that makes us feel feelings.
Roads are dark and America's long.

And I mean this wasn't *poetry*, these texts.
This wasn't like, y'know . . . *(Tries to remember a verse of a poem,
can't)* . . . *poetry*.

"Thinkin Of You."

"How's Things."

"Yer Check Came Today."

"Off to Bed."

"Goodnight."

That little buzz in my pocket or on the nightstand, that's the
rope gets tossed down to you at the bottom of that well. When
the thoughts come. Y'know. The Thoughts. That loneliness. The
texts, they're like, climb on up outta there, y'know. Get up outta
those thoughts, y'know, cuz "Thinkin Of You."

Truckers got wild imaginations.
Lots of time to think.
Just not much time to do much with all we been thinkin
except what don't take time at all.
And what's cheap.
(Toasts) Salud.
(Remembers, re-toasts) Na zdrowie.* She taught me that.

(Sips his drink.)

---

* Pronounced *naz drove-yeah*. See Note on Casting.

And sleep. And we sleep.
If we can.

So I started
textin her.
After she
passed.
Like every few days.
"Thinkin Of You."

"Off to Bed."

"Hope Yer Well."

. . .

"Miss You."

I'd lie a little too.

"Job hunt's goin good."

And joke.

"My love to Jesus."

"Slip in a good word."

. . .

"What are you wearing."

It was nice.
To talk.
To think of her, I mean.
It was just a nice thing that happened.

I owe you another, by the way. For the gloom.

(Tries to change the subject / mood:)

So I was hopin that, for like community service, they'd gimme a gig that was around people. Like bringin food to old people or like, bein in plays. Walkin puppies, somethin like that. Brushin cats. But I'm painting fences in Livingston.
Humane Society's full up.
So now my phone's got all this paint and shit on it now, on the cover. "Thinkin Of You."

. . .

I prolly shouldn't be here. At uh, at St. Mazie's here. In uh, in Williamsburg here. All you young people here. With yer fashions. With yer . . . Pabst.

Prolly shouldn't be here.

(Sips his drink.)

This is seltzer, this.

For now.

It's maybe not good for me, right now, to be here.
Too close, y'know how sometimes you get so close? You just get a little too close? Moths, man. Like a moth. I know I shouldn't be here but I'm, tonight I'm, I'm comin home from paintin fences, right? Take the train. Bus. Walk. I'm home. Shower. Eat. Like usual now. Alone. And I'm sittin in my house, my apartment, my home, and I'm lookin at the boxes. All the boxes. Of her stuff. And I'm thinkin how this was her mug. Her bowl she liked. The chair. And I'm tempted. Not gonna lie. I'm tempted as all fuckin fuck. Not even seven yet. Places will be open. Stores. And, even if

they're not, then bars. I can do whatever I want. I remember I can
do what I want cuz why not, actually. Actually, why the fuck not.

And that's when the phone buzzes.
On the table.

I didn't scream.
But shit I jumped.

. . .

"Thinkin Of You
too."

. . .

I may or may not have pissed myself at that moment.

It's my wife.

It's comin from my wife.

Her number.

Her number

My wife!

Fuckin, fuckin Ani! Ania Łucja Skowrońska-Torres*! My wife!!

And then I realize
I realize
her number
they gave away her number.

---

* See Note on Casting.

She's officially gone.

. . .

And I'm straight-up tempted right then.
Why not.
It's not even seven.
Why not.

Buzz.

Thing buzzes again.

"Where are you?"

I wonder how long this person's got my messages for. I wonder if
I should be embarrassed. I sent her a picture one time. *(Not that
kinda picture, buddy)* Of a fence I painted.
I don't remember everything I said.

Buzz.

"I'm at St. Mazie's."

This is not my wife this is not my wife I know cuz *cmon* this is not
my wife I wanna make that clear to you that I don't think this.

But

In that moment?

In that moment, I was comforted to know she's with the good
guys. With St. Mazie.
And that heaven is Catholic.

Buzz.

"It's a bar."

Buzz.

"In BK."

(Looks confused.)

The fuck is——?

Buzz.

"Brooklyn."
Thank you.

Buzz.

(Makes a judgmental face for Williamsburg.)

"Williamsburg."

Buzz.

"You?"

. . .

Buzz.

. . .

"You?"

. . .

It's seven o'clock in Bayonne. The snow just started fallin.

And I wonder what to do.
This is not my wife this is not Ani my wife.

But

But honestly, I dunno what else to do.
Except I *do*, I do know what else to do.
I always know what else I COULD do.
But maybe
maybe something . . .
the shit that happens is not to be understood
and so maybe I should get some fuckin pants on and GO.

I'm in a cab (okay my car don't tell nobody).
I'm on the PATH.
I'm on the L. (The L!)
I'm here.

I'm here.

(He takes in the Williamsburg bar.)

And nobody looks like my wife.

Or at me.

Except you.

Yer
Yer real nice.
Yer a real nice guy, man.

I ain't been buzzed yet, texted, since, so. So maybe whoever it, y'know, she's gone.

Man. A ghost ever stood YOU up, man?

Shit listen to me. The GLOOM. That's number three. Yer killin me here. Get a drink. On me. No no no don't even think about passin, man. I owe you.
My treat.

(He tries to catch a bartender, who ignores him, passes him by. He looks back at his guest.)

Y'know what though? Whoever it is, was, Miss Mazie Saint Mazie or whatever this place is, fuckin, I hope she's havin a good night. I say that genuinely, man. Even though she stood me up. The punk. I'm playin. I hope she found someone here and ended up she's havin a real good night right now. Whatever that means to her. I hope she found someone to share the night with. That's important. Seemed like she really needed someone to talk to. It's important.

Go ahead, man. Drink's on me. Made a promise to myself. A penalty. You get just one more drink for all I put you through. Go ahead, I'm payin.

. . .

Please?

One

Early September.
It's raining outside.

An accessible apartment in Princeton. A well-kempt and rich one.

Jess stands alone, a bit nervous. But hiding it. She wears a soaked hoodie and jeans / sweats. First-generation child of an immigrant. Does not come from wealth, nor does she try to seem it. Has a hard time keeping her feelings and opinions to herself. Which has gotten her in trouble. Still, she can't help it. Or doesn't want to. She will put up a fight when she needs—and sometimes even when she doesn't or perhaps shouldn't. Can take care of herself. Though perhaps wishes this were not always the case.

It's been a while. And she feels very foreign here.

JESS

Nice apartment.

(No response. She waits.
She judges his nice apartment.)

Should I be——?

JOHN

(From off) Hold on.

JESS

Cuz I could——*[tidy or]*

JOHN

(From off, "stop talking") Can't hear you.

JESS

Is there somethin you want me to do?, while yer——

(Flush, offstage.)

Cuz I would never take advantage of the hourly rate, if I were hired. Not, y'know, doin anything while yer——in there.

(John enters in a wheelchair.

He is beautiful.

John has cerebral palsy.
A kind of halted way of speaking.
Otherwise, he is determinedly polished.
Comes from wealth and wears it, undeniably.

Jess had prepared for this. Had prepared to look unphased.
But she is. She is phased.
And he is beautiful.

He looks her over a while before speaking.)

JOHN
Do you have a problem being alone?

. . .

JESS
No.

JOHN
You would get to think a lot. Waiting's
part of the job.

JESS
Sorry, I never worked with the, Differently Abled—

JOHN
Don't do that.

JESS
What?

JOHN
Don't call it that.

JESS
Why, I—

JOHN
Don't call it different
-ly abled.

JESS
Shit is that not the right term?

JOHN
It's
fucking retarded.

. . .

JESS

So what do I How do I, *refer* to you?

JOHN

Are you planning on talking about me?

JESS

No.

JOHN

Why not?
I'm very interesting.

. . .

JESS

(*Referring to the bathroom*) So after you, y'know, then would I have
to . . . ?

JOHN

Why do you want
this job?

JESS

I thought,
the experience and I—it'd be a very Meaningful Experience—

JOHN

Why do you want—

JESS

The money.

JOHN

Good.

JESS

And I'd be good at it. I'm responsible.

JOHN

Oh good. So you wouldn't
lose me.
Have you ever washed someone before?

JESS

Yeah.

JOHN

You have?

JESS

Yeah.

JOHN

(Dubious assessment)

JESS

(Not meek, but clearly not a story she cares to share) You need me to
like, describe it?

JOHN

How much can you lift? Think you can
lift me?

Hundred and forty-five pounds.

Wet.

JESS

I can lift you.

JOHN

You don't need to
bench-press me. You would help lift me out of my chair, and onto
my
shower seat. Then you
wash me. Every morning. My hair. Teeth. Trim my
whiskers, on occasion.
You'd keep me handsome.

*(John reaches a shaky hand out to Jess. She hands him her résumé.
He takes it, with two hands, and unfolds it—possibly partly with his
mouth—and smooths it out on his thighs. Looks at it. Judges.)*

JESS

Whatever I haven't done, I'd figure it out.

JOHN

And this is all
present employment?

JESS

Yeah.

JOHN

A lot of
present employment.

JESS

(A quiet dig) Fer some people. Yeah.

JOHN

These are late bars?

JESS

What?

JOHN

(Impatient) These are late bars, bars that
stay open late, that you // work at?

JESS

Depends but. Yeah. Yes. They're open late.
(Suddenly realizing) I understood you It wasn't cuz I couldn't The
way you How you Your um—
Yeah they're open late.

(John looks back down at the résumé.)

I'd set an alarm.

JOHN

You went here?

JESS

Where?

JOHN

To school. Here.

JESS

Yeah.
I went here. Few years ago. Fer undergrad.

Why wouldn't I.

JOHN

So why are you still here? In
September. At the start of the school year. If you
graduated.

JESS

Fer this job.

JOHN

Interview.

JESS

Fer this job interview.

JOHN

Curious.

JESS

What.

JOHN

That you're here for *this* kind of job.
If you graduated from / / Prince—

JESS

I graduated.
With honors.

JOHN

It doesn't say on the— What / / did you study—?

JESS

I'm just lookin for a side job. Somethin extra. For on the side.

JOHN

In addition to all the— / / cocktail wait—?

JESS

It's a loud as fuck alarm.

. . .

And you?, yer here for . . . *(Trying to guess his age)* . . . / / college?

JOHN

PhD.
Graduate School.
For Political Science. Just moved here.
From *Cambridge*.

(He waits for her to be impressed.
She's giving him nothing.
On purpose.)

Near Boston.

(Nothing.)

. . . Massachu—

JESS

Harvard.

JOHN

Since you mention it.

(John judges the résumé. Jess gets nervous.)

JESS

Listen whatever I haven't done, I'd figure it out—

JOHN

How much life have you lived?

JESS

I'm . . . twenty-five—

JOHN

Numbers don't
interest me. How much life
have you seen?
Not everyone can do this work.

JESS

Why? You make shit hard fer people?

JOHN

This "shit" can, by nature, be hard. Not everyone can
cut it. I don't hire from agencies; so some
applicants think they can do it and then it turns out
they can't.

JESS

How come you don't hire from agencies?

JOHN

I don't have to.

JESS

Why not.

JOHN

I have money. I can basically do
anything I want except the things I
can't.

JESS

What's wrong with agencies?

JOHN

They don't appreciate my lawsuits.

If their people mess up, I can sue them so
agencies limit aides to just
doing the basics.

JESS

. . . What kinda stuff goes beyond the basics?

JOHN

You ask a lot of // questions.

JESS

What might you be havin me do that's not the basics?

JOHN

Various things. // I don't have a—

JESS

But what would I—

JOHN

If you don't interrupt me—because, you see, it can take me a
minute—
if you don't interrupt me, you'll get
all the information you need.

JESS

Sorry.

JOHN

Forgiven. I don't have a list but things come up. You do whatever
I need,
within reason. You *would*, I mean, if you were hired.
You'll have to pardon my,
well,
suspicion but you're not what
usually applies for this job.

JESS

And "what" usually applies?

JOHN

Oh you know.

JESS

(She does) No. Please tell me.

JOHN

I need someone who can really do this work so if you're
not willing to—
I'm sorry but—

JESS

A lot.

JOHN

What?

JESS

Of life.
Is how much I've lived.
So when a man tells me I'd hafta do some Various Things for him
for money, I gotta push that man for a little clarity.

JOHN

Okay.
Well when a woman says she went to Prince—

JESS

Cuz she did. She did. She says it, she writes it in her résumé, cuz
she did. She went to school, she's lived a lot of life—before and
after school—and she could do this. I could do this. If yer surprised I'd be applyin for a job like this, while workin a buncha
jobs like those *(Referring to the résumé)*, after goin to a place like
this *(Referring to school)*, then sorry, bro—

JOHN

John.

JESS

If a man like you—

JOHN

// Like what.

JESS

—livin how you do—

JOHN

And how's that?

JESS

If you don't understand why where I went to school, *that* I went to school, doesn't mean shit for some people—then I dunno what yer payin for in there.

JOHN

I'm fully funded // actually—

JESS

But I am not yer professor. Yer professor gets health insurance.

JOHN

Not necessarily—

JESS

I'd do whatever, okay?, whatever you needed.
I'd do whatever.
John.
Within reason.

Sorry—sorry I interrupted you.

(John looks at her.)

Please.

(John looks back down at the résumé.

It might look at first like defeat.
Perhaps Jess turns toward the door.

He looks back up.)

                    JOHN
Jess.

                    JESS
Yeah?

                    JOHN
-ica?

                    JESS
Just Jess.

                    JOHN
Early riser, *Jess*?

                    JESS
Can be.

                    JOHN
Six A.M.?

                    JESS
(Lying) . . . Yup.

JOHN

Well then.

(He extends his hand to her.
A moment.
She watches it shake.

Then
she shakes his hand.)

Here we go.

Two

Early September.
It's raining outside.

A different accessible apartment. In Jersey City, New Jersey. A largely empty one, in transition and under-loved.

A woman enters. Ani.
She is in a wheelchair. Severe incomplete spinal cord injury.
Quadriplegic. Though some of the fingers of one hand are partially functioning.
Ani is a woman whose world has not extended very far beyond North Jersey and just you try to say something to her and watch what happens. She has her own ways and she is fine with those ways and those that do not agree don't need to stick around—as many haven't. She can seem brusque or intense to some people. A cat that resists being pet. Until it wants to be.

Eddie enters with her, holding an umbrella over her. Then remembers the umbrella:

EDDIE

Oh shit.
Bad luck.

(Eddie closes the umbrella. Sets it aside.
Their interactions used to have ease. Eddie muscles it now.)

So this is yer new . . .

(He is surprised at the place. Takes it in.)

Ani.

You need to get some color in here. *(The worst)* This beige? No.
Feel like I'm walkin into a paper bag. You could get some kinda
yellow in here. Some baby blue, some yellow. Good for emotions. I read that. It's therapy. Colors work on yer feelings. Blue's
for stress, like—relief. Red's for passion. And yellow I dunno
but it's *yellow*.
Ask yer nurses. Watch. They'll tell you. Shit's science.

ANI

(Bone dry) I thought I'd try yoga.
Fer my emotions.

EDDIE

. . . Can you // do—?

ANI

NO.

EDDIE

Okay.

(He looks around for something helpful to do.)

ANI

What're you doin // here—?

EDDIE

(Looking for tasks) OkayOkayOkay. Pillow! Got yer pillow here.

(He tries to put it somewhere behind her head or back. Sees she's strapped in all over . . .)

I'ma just fluff THAT.

(. . . Fluffs and sets the pillow aside.)

Okay. Blanket. Just blanket you with THAT.

(He tucks a blanket around her chair.)

You lose weight?

. . .

I will punch myself later for that. On yer behalf.

Or— Y'know what:

*(He takes her paralyzed arm.
She's confused at what's going on at first but has no control over it.
Oh no. Is he really doing this?
He is. He's really doing this. She can't believe he's doing this.*

He punches himself with her paralyzed hand.

She doesn't look happy.)

He sees her face, not looking happy.

And he awkwardly puts her hand back down by her side.)

ANI

The fuck is wrong // with you?

EDDIE

I don't know.

ANI

Strap it back in!

EDDIE

Sorry sorry.

(He straps her wrist back on the arm of the chair.)

ANI

Flatten it out.

EDDIE

What?

ANI

My fingers, you gotta— Flatten // out my— Or I'll lose those too.

EDDIE

Right.

(He returns her hand to pre-fist position, flattening her fingers on the palm pad of her chair.)

There you go.
You good?

37

ANI

Don't I look it?
What the fuck are you // doin here?—

EDDIE

The bed's the wrong way.

ANI

What?

EDDIE

Yer bed's faced away from the window.

ANI

Leave it.

EDDIE

Lemme move the bed.

ANI

Leave it.

EDDIE

Lemme just do this real // quick.

ANI

(Finality) NO, Eddie.
Just— // leave it.

EDDIE

Sorry. I do that.

ANI

Okay?

EDDIE

Okay.

ANI

Okay?

EDDIE

Okay.
Damn

ANI

But thank you.

EDDIE

(Sass) You *would be* welcome.

ANI

Why were you just standin outside my place // in the rain like some—?

EDDIE

I'm just sayin' you could get yerself some light. Ani. By the window. Light's good. Keeps you happy. Serotonin. Vitamins. There is vitamins in the sun that's only in the sun that—and we need it. So listen, it gets cloudy or rainy or some shit like this again 'n'see if they'll get you a box.
One a those boxes with the light comin from it.
Get one 'n' put it by yer face.
It's for serotonin.
It's supposed to shoot like, serotonin at yer face.
When there's none outside.

It's prob'ly covered in yer plan.
'N' if not, you lemme know.

ANI

I'm still on yer plan.

EDDIE

Right.

ANI

So you'll know.
You'll know if I need a box.
To keep me happy.

EDDIE

True.

ANI

We can figure all that out, the insurance, soon's the papers—

EDDIE

We don't gotta // talk about that right now.

ANI

I'm just sayin that for now I'm on yer plan. Til the papers.

EDDIE

We can hold off on the papers. I'm sayin if you need. Fer the insurance.
They're just papers.

ANI

They're a lot more than that.

. . .

Why are you here.

EDDIE

You look into that stuff I sent you?

ANI

What stuff?

EDDIE

I emailed you! Good stuff. Cuz those guys you go to?, they can move yer arms fer you, y'know, stretch you out or whatever they do on like the *physical* level, but there's other kinds of therapies you can do. They're prob'ly just givin you the basics over there.

ANI

So I should paint my fuckin walls is what yer sayin.
Then I'm cured.

EDDIE

Listen I have seen Miraculous Shit on YouTube. Actually, on the whole internet. It's good to have in yer back pocket, y'know, cuz insurance, my insurance, won't always . . . y'know.

ANI

You tryin to get rid of me?

EDDIE

What?

ANI

Off yer insurance? // Fast as you can? That's why yer here?

EDDIE

What?, no! I'm—no, man! All I'm sayin's maybe colors! Yellows. Blues. That's all I'm sayin. I dunno if you knew about em so I'm, now you know about em.
(Like he's not allowed to say it) I . . . I've been thinkin about you.

41

ANI

When?

EDDIE

What?

ANI

Was it when I went unconscious from the sepsis? Was it then? When I woke up from the surgery. The second surgery. Or when they said I need one more. Maybe it was May. The day I learned to move a finger. Or was it just September. When I find you standin at my door. When exactly, Eddie, in the last six months since I saw you after the accident, did you think to think of me?

. . .

EDDIE

I wasn't sure you wanted to see me.

ANI

What in the world would give you that idea.

. . .

. . .

EDDIE

There's also this thing I read says certain smells, right, // could—

ANI

I know.

EDDIE

You don't even know what I was gonna say.

ANI

That shit's not real.

EDDIE

What shit.

ANI

Colors. Smells. All that. Not real.

EDDIE

I dunno, I seen on YouTube—

ANI

Okay well my nurse is comin by at seven—

EDDIE

Oh cool good *cool*. So *she* / / can tell you—

ANI

So you can go. You can go.
Thanks fer . . . settin me up.
I'm all set up now.
All set.

EDDIE

Yer welcome.

ANI

Bye.

EDDIE

Except . . .

ANI

What?

EDDIE

I texted you . . . about . . .

43

ANI

What?

EDDIE

There's just one // thing—

ANI

WHAT.

EDDIE

Except I gotta get my stuff?
I still gotta get some more of my stuff?

. . .

I texted? Last week. You, yer nurse, musta accidentally packed some of *my* stuff. I texted you about me comin by at some point to get my stuff. I called too. You ain't answer so—

ANI

So get yer stuff.

EDDIE

But I—okay—this is funny—so I kinda left forgot my, the, suit-cases . . . at—

ANI

I don't have any suitcases.

EDDIE

So some are comin by.

ANI

Some . . . suitcases are comin by?

EDDIE

In a few.

ANI

Just . . . rollin by?

EDDIE

In a car.

ANI

She can't come in here.

. . .

EDDIE

You want me just to wait outside?

ANI

Yes I do.

EDDIE

("Yer right") Okay.
. . .
. . .
In the rain?

ANI

Do what you want.

EDDIE

But like but what would you *prefer*?

ANI

Do what you want.

EDDIE

Okay.

ANI

Fuckin, *prefer*.

EDDIE

I'll wait right here then.

ANI

Then wait here.

EDDIE

Okay.

(He waits.)

Want me to put on some music?

ANI

What is wrong with you?

EDDIE

No, not like—not like . . . *[sexy]* . . . *music*. Like . . . fer therapy.
// I read—

ANI

No.

EDDIE

Okay but yer not supposed to do like, homework or somethin,
some kinda physical therapy homework? After yer appointments?

ANI

You didn't read about it? On the whole internet?

EDDIE

How can I help? Ani. While I'm here, how can I help?

ANI

You don't gotta help me with shit. We're separated. Congratulations on yer suitcases.

. . .

EDDIE

I'll wait outside.

(Ani watches——or senses——him walk toward the door.)

ANI

Sometimes they give you . . . physical therapy homework.

(Eddie turns back.)

EDDIE

Like what?

ANI

(Bone dry) Like "Try to move."
They do say I should listen to music.

EDDIE

See, I was tryin to tell you about that. And you'll do that?

ANI

It's not—

EDDIE

Do that. It works. I dunno how—they don't explain in the video—
// but just *listen* to it—

47

ANI

I'm about to say some shit to you, Eddie, 'n' I want you to hear it, okay?, so here's a Notice, an Advanced fuckin, that I'm about to say some shit I want you to hear. Okay?
You listening?

EDDIE

. . . Yeah.

ANI

Don't interrupt me.

EDDIE

Yeah okay go.

ANI	EDDIE
I'm sad 'n' I'm gonna—	You want the music?

(Let's try that again.)

I'm sad 'n' I'm gonna—	You don't want the music?
I'M SAD	

ANI

'N' pissed. 'N' I'm gonna be sad, pissed 'n' sad, fer however long I'm pissed 'n' sad, 'n' that's fine. I feel like feelin whatever I feel right now. In my paper bag. 'N' that's fine.

There's no recovery from this.
My spinal cord's shattered. This: Is it.
I know you know that so please just . . . don't. Okay?

I can mail you yer shit.
I mean not *me*. I can't, fuckin— But somehow I, yer shit will be mailed. The nurse can mail em.
I'll consider that box fer my face.

(She sees Eddie on his phone.)

Are you // listening?

(Suddenly, music.
Eddie plays some music from his phone.
Upbeat. And way too loud.)

EDDIE
How can you be sad with THIS?!?

(He dances.

He's having a GREAT time.

He tries to involve her

and then

eventually

he realizes how shitty that makes him
that he's dancing
and she can't.

And he stops.
The music still plays.)

I can paint the walls // fer you.

ANI
Turn it off.

EDDIE
It's therapy, it can—

ANI

It's not. That's not therapy. Turn it off.

(He turns it off.)

. . .

You still can't dance.

. . .
. . .
. . .

EDDIE

Look who's talkin.

. . .
. . .
. . .

(They look at each other.
And crack.
Laughter.
We can see why they were once good together.

There's a moment where they stop laughing.
And recognize that. And maybe this is both a good and bad thing.
Ani puts down her abrasion for a moment.)

ANI

The way the therapist explained it

music

if you really wanna know

EDDIE

I'm listening.

*(She has had no one with which to share new information.
It's a vulnerable act. And he is listening.)*

ANI

. . . is when music plays, the body goes lookin for the things it's missing. The broken things. The shit that's disconnected. And it tries to bring everything back together. Like it used to be. Back in order. Order like . . . music.
(A dig, before he can contest her) Classical shit.

The PT's helped me to *(She indicates she's moving her finger)* a little, and just on that hand, but the music's supposed to . . .

You listen and . . .

(She moves the fingers of one hand as if playing piano.)

yer body tries to imitate the . . . sense that music makes // which is why—

*(Beep-beep.
Car horn outside.*

There she is. The end of all that.)

Can I just—can I just mail the stuff, Eddie?

EDDIE

That's expensive.

ANI

I'd rather mail it.

EDDIE

I'll just go get the bags // and—

ANI

I got an emergency button on this thing. I'll press the shit out of
it I swear.

EDDIE

Who do you*[think I am?]*, cmon. You don't gotta threaten me //
like I'm some kinda, fuckin—

ANI

I'm askin you then, then I'm askin you: Can I mail yer stuff.
Say yes.

(He hovers by the door.)

EDDIE

I'll send you the list. A list. Of my stuff.

ANI

Is she livin with you?
. . . In our . . . ? In . . . Bayonne?

EDDIE

No.

ANI

Will she?

. . .

EDDIE

(Caught) . . . it's just cheaper fer us both to, instead of—

ANI

("No more") Okay.

EDDIE

I can't pay fer a place on my own and help you at the same time.

ANI

I'll pay it back.

EDDIE

(Not unkindly) Yeah but
but I'm payin it now.

. . .

ANI

She's patient.

EDDIE

What?

ANI

Only beeped once.

EDDIE

I should head out.

ANI

Yeah.
Maybe you should.

EDDIE

Ani—

(He decides not to say whatever he was gonna say.)

Don't worry about the stuff. Fuck the stuff, it's not important.

ANI

Which stuff?

EDDIE

It's nothin I can't live without.

(Eddie wonders if this is goodbye for a while.)

Bye, Ani.

(He hovers by the door,

sees if she'll look at him.

She doesn't.

And exits.

Ani, alone.

Silence.

She takes in that she's alone.

. . .
. . .

She closes her eyes.

A finger moves.

The fingers of one hand move.

As if playing piano. Or trying to.

She plays an invisible piano with a few of her fingers on one hand.

. . .

We watch her in silence.

. . .

Then, car engine.

A car drives away.

She opens her eyes.

No one.)

Three

September. Early morning.
John's apartment.
Jess's first day at work.

Jess prepares to shave John's face.

JESS

You tell me if I fuck up.

JOHN

If you
fuck up, you'll know.

(Jess moves the razor to his face.
About to do it but—)

Don't fuck up.

(About to do it but——)

Tired?

JESS

There's a knife in my hand.

(A breath, gets ready) Okay.

(She shaves him.
When the razor is far from his face——)

JOHN

Was it a long night?
At the bar?

(She shaves him. Hesitantly.)

JESS

Yup.

JOHN

Me too. Long night.
Had a paper to write.
Tired?

JESS

(Lying) Nope.

JOHN

I am.

JESS

It's not the same.

JOHN

What.

JESS

(Referring to the shaving) It's hard to do this when yer talkin.

JOHN

I'm not
contagious.

JESS

What? I know.

JOHN

So come closer.

(She does.)

"The better to see you with, my dear."

JESS

. . . What?

JOHN

Nothing.

(She shaves him.)

I hired an English major who doesn't talk.

JESS

Who said I was an—

JOHN

Why else not list your
major? On your résumé.
Art history.

JESS

No.

JOHN

Ceramics.

JESS

No.

JOHN

Then tell me something
about yourself.

JESS

So you can make fun of me?

JOHN

No.
Depends.
Tell me something.

JESS

I can tell you I ain't cut you yet. I can tell you that.

JOHN

You're about to
see a lot of me. To know a lot of me.
You will take off my clothes and I will have nowhere to hide.
I don't really have a choice in that.

JESS

You had the choice to hire me.

JOHN

And my choices don't stop there.
Every morning you walk in here, I have a choice about that.

It would be nice to know
who is taking off my clothes.

JESS

You want a story?

JOHN

Or a vase. If that's how you
express.

JESS

I work at a bar. I drive there. In a car. Then I drive away.
I work at another bar. Take the train there, then I take the train back.
I work at bars. What do you want me to say? I went to college. This
one. And I work at a bar.
Bars.
The End.

JOHN

I'm just trying to talk.

JESS

Well I'm not my favorite thing to talk about.

JOHN

Why not—

JESS

You gonna tell me to smile fer you next?

JOHN

No—

JESS

Smile, sweetheart.

JOHN

// No—

JESS

(Wipes his face with a towel) I think yer good. No blood.

(Jess moves away from John.
Perhaps John sits there a moment.
Alone. For just a moment.)

JOHN

(Kindly, one more try) Where are you from?

JESS

Okay what's next. Shower. Right. I shower you next.

(No response.)

(Takes it upon herself to try to manipulate his chair) Okay, let's go—

(John moves himself away from her.)

JOHN

You want to just get it over with?

JESS

. . . What?

JOHN

You don't like to talk about yourself— Or to me— And you're
clearly— So let's just get this all out of the way.
The last thing I want to be reminded of every
morning, first thing in the—is how
uncomfortable my
body // makes—

JESS

I am not uncomfortable.

JOHN

Really?
Because I am.

JOHN
(Continuing) The knees and
elbows can't stop drawing / /
towards each other. I fight to
keep them apart. The joints
feel like magnets—
Try it.

JESS
I am not uncomfortable with
yer—I feel perfectly—
Did I mess anything up?
Cuz I don't think I messed
anything up.

JESS

Try what.

JOHN

What it would feel like.
Your knees and elbows—

JESS

Like pretend to be—Are you askin me to make fun of you?

JOHN

You are making fun of me
by thinking you'd be making fun of me.
It's part of the job.

JESS

The job's to shave you, shower you, brush yer teeth, to / / get yer—

JOHN

To take care of my body. Right. To understand me and
the needs of my body. That's your job.

JESS

And how's imitating you gonna help me shave yer face?

JOHN

I'm not asking you to—
Okay.
Okay.
Maybe this. Maybe you
maybe this just isn't working // out.

JESS

No, okay— Fuck— Look, I just started—

JOHN

If you treat me like a job—

JESS

You *are* my job.

JOHN

Like I'm not even—

JESS

You'd fire me cuz I don't wanna, what, mock you?

JOHN

No, // I'm not asking you to—

JESS

(Continuing) Cuz I didn't entertain you // on command?

JOHN

No, just—

JESS

I am not uncomfortable—

JOHN

(At the frustrated end of his rope) Then why can't we have a human
conversation.

This was a mistake.

JESS

Most people assume my name's Jessica.

It's not.

My mother came to the country with no English, very little, and
she's in this hospital in Newark—it's not there anymore this is
clearly like a few years—and the nurse hands me to my mom for
the first time. She was here alone. No family. And the nurse asks
my mom like, what'll you call her? And my mom just looks at
her. She said that's the moment it hit her, how alone she is. How
little English. How everything now it's hers. Her shoulders. And
she thought the nurse said— When my mom was asked a ques-
tion, she'd usually either just say yes or no or okay like judgin on
if it was a man or a woman she was answerin, or if they looked
nice, I mean most times people just asked her like, do you want a
bag or are you okay and so she says yes or no or I'm okay. And so
my mom, when the nurse asked my name, she I think she meant
to say yes but, in her, y'know, her accent . . .

So my name's Jess.

Just Jess.

They were nice enough to put two s's.

. . .

JOHN

You tell everyone that story? That's your
story, right?, that you tell everyone?

JESS

Y'know what how bout I just finish the job and you can judge me
on that. So shower. // I'll shower you now.

JOHN

I didn't mean to judge you—

(Jess reaches carelessly for John's shirt, as if to undress him.
The surprising, forceful contact causes John to spasm and splay.
Jess pulls away, instinct.
John risks falling out of the chair but catches himself.
Jess freezes, doesn't know what to do.

Throughout the following, John recovers.
At some point Jess assists him in a small way.)

My body—
if you get too close, too fast—

My body overprotects itself.

Anytime I reach beyond myself,
it's violence.
You reach and you shake and
it always feels beyond you.
So you have to throw yourself—your
arms, your hands—at what you want.

(He grabs her arm.
Holds her.)

Have you ever been hit?

. . .

Have you ever been—

JESS

Why.

JOHN

That's what it's like. Under my skin. From underneath
my skin. Like people hitting me
from beneath my skin.

(He lets her go.)

And that's what you'll be working with. Every morning. Is touching,
shaving,
undressing,
washing
and clothing—that.
That's what I'm like.

(They stand apart a moment.)

JESS

That the story *you* tell everyone?

JOHN

No, actually.
No one ever asks.

JESS

Well I clearly wasn't gonna.

JOHN

And I don't like to talk about it.

JESS

Why did you?

JOHN

Because I never did.

You're the
first, my
first
I ever hired on my own.
Since I started living on my own.

I never . . .

*(Something feels unsatisfactory to John.
He goes back to logistics.)*

There's an aftershave lotion
you can use.

JESS

What else you never done?

JOHN

What?

JESS

You said you never . . . so . . .
What else, John, have you never done?

(Something new is beginning.)

Tell me something
about yourself.

Four

October.
Evening. Ani's apartment.

ANI

Hell no.

EDDIE

But I know you, yer body—

ANI

More reason fer No. You knew how fuckin amazing it *was*.

EDDIE

I need the money.

ANI

Why? Fer her?

EDDIE

No. Fer like, in general.

Cmon, you'd rather have a stranger, some kinda—stranger comin in to take care of you? You don't know people, Ani.

ANI

I knew *you* 'n' see what happened?

EDDIE

Y'know it's really hard to talk to you when all you got is trumps on me.

ANI

I'm not hiring you.

EDDIE

Discrimination.

ANI

Fine. Cuff me.

EDDIE

You wouldn't hafta pay me as much as someone else.

ANI

How's what's-her-fuck feel about this?

EDDIE

Great.

ANI

She has no idea.

EDDIE

No, we definitely communicated about it. You really got a button?

ANI

What? / / Yes I do.

EDDIE

An emergency button, you got one? Then press it.

ANI

No.

EDDIE

Press it.

ANI

No.

EDDIE

Press it.

ANI

No!

EDDIE

Press it if you don't want me here.
Press it.

ANI

I really gotta say, Eddie, that I never got as huge an urge to get the
fuck outta this chair as when I saw yer fuckin face. Since I seen
you last month? The weaponry that's been dancin in my dreams,
the violence that I would like to do to you is so—creative that
that's when I feel like I could just vault outta my body. Outta this
chair. Those moments are my most alive.

EDDIE

So hire me.

. . .

You been thinkin about me?

ANI

What?

EDDIE

Since "last month."

(Perhaps he sings / dances a bit, as in their first scene.)

ANI

Get the fuck outta my house.

EDDIE

Ani, whatever I don't understand now about . . . I will. I learn fast. Just gimme a week. Just gimme a trial run fer like, a week.

ANI

Yer here cuz you feel like a fuck.

EDDIE

I always felt like a fuck. I'm just variations of that feeling from day to day.

ANI

And when you quit feelin like the lowest of a fuck, however or whoever makes you feel even half a rung higher, then you'll leave. I know you.

EDDIE

You know that One Time that happened.

ANI

Yer *livin* with her in our place in Bayonne, that's more than once.

EDDIE

We were separating. At the time, the first time, you 'n' I were—
We're // separated!

ANI

Right. I know you.

EDDIE

That's right. That's right you do know me. You know me as a man
who's been twelve years sober. A man who's been twenty—almost
one—years faithful. I wasn't some perfect // fuckin y'know, but—

ANI

Yup.

EDDIE

But I was pretty good, Ani. You can't deny the numbers. Twelve.
Twenty almost one.
Not spotless, especially with the—but pretty good. Shit, compared
to—

ANI

What.
Me?

EDDIE

To before.
Compared to *me* before. Twelve years ago 'n' then the nine before
that? Compared to that, I done pretty good. That part I don't
need you to confirm fer me. I know that. I know I got far. I know
that in like, myself. That I come a long way. With that shit?, with
me before?, a *week* is far.
(A quiet truth) Proud of that. So.
I've taken care of you before. When you were goin through //
yer own—

ANI

(Not proud of this, "stop talking") Okay.

EDDIE

Not tryin to hold that over you. I know what that is, to hafta be taken care of. I'm just sayin . . . you seen my work.

ANI

Yer what?

EDDIE

You woke up the next day. You ain't die. So I guess that's my like, work sample. Yer my work sample.

ANI

I was blacked-out fer most of yer work sample.

EDDIE

Like I said, you ain't die.
Look, how much money you actually have to spend? How much would this cost you to get someone—?

ANI

I get checks. And I've applied for // some things.

EDDIE

And all the hidden costs? I got a nice fat report from the internet about THAT.

ANI

I'd rather find some way to pay someone than just hang on yer insurance forever like a fuckin, or onto you—

EDDIE

How? // How would you—?

ANI

I dunno, man, but I'd rather do that!

EDDIE

And go a few days without bathing? Having brushed teeth? Eating?

ANI

I'd rather find someone I can trust—

EDDIE

Like yer nurse tonight?

ANI

This is one time This is one time this is happened She had her schedule wrong probably she probably had her schedule wrong.

EDDIE

Just this one time, she fucked up. This the only time?

ANI

Just this time.

EDDIE

And yer okay with that? Yer okay with that? You'd trust her again? To show up? To do what she's gotta do?

ANI

. . .

EDDIE

Just once.
Like me.

ANI

What do you think's gonna happen you come take care of me a few hours a day? Huh? You brush my teeth a couple mornings, dump my bedpan a few times and BOOM, consc*[ience]*—fuck-shit, clap yer hands when I say Boom.

EDDIE

What?

ANI

You dump my bedpan and
BOOM—clap yer hands.

EDDIE

Like, // applause—?

ANI

CLAP. Like one clap.
And BOOM, clap yer—CLAP YER—

(He claps.)

Not yet! Aaaand BOOM—

(He claps.)

Aaaand BOOM.

(He claps on BOOM.)

And BOOM—

(He claps on BOOM.)

And BOOM—

(He claps on BOOM.)

And BOOM *(He claps)* and BOOM *(He claps)* and BOOM *(He claps)*—You dump my bedpan a few times and BOOM *(He claps)*—conscience cleared?

. . .

EDDIE

. . . This what you did with yer nurse? Maybe this is why she ditched you.

ANI

Yer not doin penance on me.

EDDIE

Yer right cuz yer not my fault. This wasn't my fault.
You right now?, the way you are? *(He claps)* Not my fault.
Look I know you won't forgive me fer the—I know that. Even though we were separated. Technically. Which, I mean maybe you'll forgive // me but— Okay.

ANI

Nope.

EDDIE

All I can hope for then, I guess, is some kinda shift. Not forgiveness I guess but. I dunno.
I can just hope fer something like that.
But I didn't do this to you. So.
So, no, I don't owe you penance for that.

I'd be doin a service. Fer free. Or at a real cheap rate, if you need that to make it feel . . . whatever.
And temporary.

ANI

. . .

EDDIE

. . .

ANI

You know what we talk about? My nurse 'n' me? What we talked
about? Nothin usually. She'd ask me how I'm doin, how this
'n' that feels. Any problems? Physical problems? The weather.
Straightforward shit like that. She tells me the weather all over
America. We sympathize over snow in Chicago. We shake our
heads at the humidity in Atlanta. We sigh about Minnesota. That
must be awful, we say. That must be so awful fer people. Wher-
ever she's got family, I know about it. I know about what their
days must be cuz she tells me their weather.
I fuckin love that bitch.

EDDIE

. . . it's still raining outside but it's supposed to // clear up
tomorrow.

ANI

And it's nice—it is sometimes real nice to just think about some-
one's weather. To feel bad fer their snow.
To forget I used to live a different way.
To forget what other people gotta do for me that I can't anymore.
That I did this to myself.

EDDIE

You didn't—
It was an acci[dent]— Bad luck.
I'm sorry.
I'll never bring that up again.

ANI

We got too many trumps on each other. Decades of em.
I can see why you'da gone to her. It's nice to talk about other
things . . . the weather . . . sometimes.
. . .
Okay, I'm done. No more of that talk.
New apartment. New body. New life. Old nurse.

EDDIE

Could I just try?

ANI

Why?

EDDIE

Cuz you don't have much of a choice in it.

ANI

. . . Why don't I?

EDDIE

Cuz I already told em I'd take care of things.

ANI

I do have a button.

EDDIE

Okay. And it went right to me.
I'm yer emergency contact.
I'm still yer emergency contact.
So when it turned out yer nurse couldn't come tonight, they called me.
I said I'd go over 'n' check on you.
I said I would
'n' I'm here.

ANI

. . . I can change those forms.

EDDIE

'N' who would you put? Who do we know in our lives who'd come? Who's got the money or the . . .*[responsibility]*. . . who you think could do this?

. . .

Can I—please—try to help you this week?
I've got a week before I hafta head out again for a drive. Seven
days.
Seven.
Just the nights.
Seven nights, starting tonight.

ANI

Why?

EDDIE

If I fuck up, I'm gone. They're findin you someone new anyways
but fer now—

ANI

But—why, Eddie?

EDDIE

Cuz I'd like to see you.

. . .

Seven nights.

. . .

Ania*?

. . .

(Something shifts for Ani.
She sees her lot.)

———
* See Note on Casting.

. . .

ANI

My birthday.

It's my birthday next month. Three weeks.

I forgot.

. . .

. . .

I'll be forty-two.

. . .

EDDIE

(As though he is the present) Happy Birthday, baby.

Five

December.
John's apartment.

Jess showers John.
We watch the entire act.
It takes as long as it needs.

Jess wheels John into the shower.
She helps lift him from his wheelchair onto his shower seat.
How this happens: John embraces Jess, who he uses as support. Jess holds
onto John as he pushes himself up and pivots on his toes from the wheel-
chair to the shower seat.
She undresses him completely.
She runs the water.
Tests it on herself.
Tests it on his arm.
He nods if the temperature's okay.

She washes his hair.
She soaps his body and rinses it off.

Jess picks up a conversation she began earlier.
There is more ease between the two now.

JESS

I mean I don't love these women either—sometimes they're worse than the but I'm not givin the girl tequila when she's that fuckin *done,* y'know.

JOHN

Naturally.

JESS

Especially when she ain't order it. I mean I'll take a man's money whatever but No Rapes On My Watch. This girl's on the couches we got, in the back, right, half dressed, half asleep (and this place is not, y'know, it's *loud*), and this guy to me he's like, YO cmere. Like, Ey-oh!, OVER HERE. And he's one of those, y'know, with the button-doooown—

JOHN

Right.

JESS

jeeeeans

JOHN

(Judgment) God.

JESS

with the hair, y'know what I'm sayin?

JOHN

Oh yes.

JESS

And orange. He tans. Bro, it's fuckin December. And he's like This girl needs a *shot*. So I'm like Listen chief I think she's *good*. And he's like Listen bitch—

JOHN

Uh-oh.

JESS

Who's got the money, he says, and who the fuck are you?

JOHN

Wow.

JESS

And he throws this balled-up dollar in my face.

JOHN

Some people.

JESS

Bouncer palmed his greasy head 'n' threw his douche-ass out.

JOHN

Good.

JESS

Right in the snow. Man, fuck rich people. No offense but heads on sticks. France should happen here.

(A moment of silent showering.)

I don't understand why people here gotta judge you by yer job. I'm not my job.

JOHN

People have to judge you by something.

JESS

Except no the fucks don't.

JOHN

How else will they know if they're
winning or not?

JESS

I don't judge people.

(John makes a judgmental noise.)

I make a sincere effort not to judge people.

JOHN

Well I hope you never drown.

JESS

I hope you never drown too, John.

JOHN

Because if it's you and Michael
Phelps and I
swimming in the Hamptons and you get a cramp? And you call on
me because you're not judgmental?
I think you'd probably die.

. . .

I judged you.

JESS

How'd you judge me?
Here, you want yer—*[wash cloth]*

JOHN

Yes please, here—

JESS

Got it?

JOHN

Got it, thanks.

(Jess puts into John's hand a soaped-up wash cloth.
He uses this to wash his genitals.
Jess turns away so he can have privacy.
It's not awkward. Routine.)

JESS

How'd you judge me?

JOHN

Well.
I think.
I judged you well,
I think.
You haven't
lost me.

(He drops the cloth on the shower floor—he's done with it.
She rinses him.)

JESS

You don't gimme the chance to lose you.
You barely leave.

JOHN

I leave.

JESS

To class, maybe.

JOHN

I don't *just* go to class.

JESS

I never see you go out.

JOHN

Big campus.

JESS

The neighborhood, even. This area. When I leave, after I'm done
here every morning, you usually just—hang.

JOHN

I don't like to be rushed.

JESS

Never see you, all I'm sayin.

JOHN

Well
I never see you.

JESS

When would you be seein me? I don't live here.
I don't even come around here except fer you.

JOHN

I—
I never see you,
except when you're working,
is all I'm saying.

86

JESS

I don't go out much.

JOHN

At all.

JESS

It's cold.

JOHN

Not all the—

JESS

Lately, yeah! Lately it's been cold as— And, man, anyways, you go out, you spend money. Coffee. Fuckin, ham sandwich. All that's money.

JOHN

So you, what,
stay home? Read? The cereal
box I guess because books are "money."

. . .

JESS

I work.

JOHN

Okay but
you can't It's not
possible to work all the—

JESS

You can. People can. They do.

JOHN

That doesn't seem like
a life.

(The silence of task-doing.)

JESS

I sleep.
For fun.

(She has placed a towel on the wheelchair.
She lifts him from his shower seat and helps situate him onto his wheelchair.
Dries his body.)

JOHN

Why— For what are you
working so much?

. . .

JESS

Everything.

(She puts on his pants. Shoes.)

(To herself) Who's got the money, he says, and who the fuck are you.

JOHN

Don't worry about that—

JESS

He's right though.

JOHN

No he's a—

COST OF LIVING

JESS

It does matter who you are.
And what you have.
It matters.

. . .

JOHN

Well
I think as long as you—

JESS

—work hard?

(She works.)

Those guys I serve at the bar? They make more in an hour—with
a finger—than I make in a week with my whole entire body.

It matters who you are. Family. Connections. If there's gonna be
a net when you fall.
Cuz everybody falls.

I'm the first one born in this country. And I'm the only one left—
I was supposed to be the one to—

I was supposed to be the net.

JOHN

Is there something going on?

JESS

I'm just exhausted.

JOHN

What's going on?

(She looks at him.

*She considers for a moment whether to tell him what's going on.
Decides against it.)*

JESS

Polo or V-neck?

JOHN

Crew, please.
The olive one.

(Jess retrieves a shirt.)

JESS

Nice. Is this another new one?

JOHN

I may have even *gone out* for it.

(She dresses him.)

JESS

So how'd you judge // me?

JOHN

What about merit?

JESS

. . . What about it?

JOHN

Aside from family and—
Doesn't merit count for something?

JESS

Depends.
On who's the judge.

JOHN

Well you're not
not-privileged either.

(Jess was about to contradict him.
Then realizes what he's referring to.)

JESS

No.
No, I'm not not-privileged either.

JOHN

And you're not
completely alone.

(Jess doesn't reply.)

You've got me in any case.

JESS

My employer.

JOHN

Your . . . well . . .

JESS

What? You pay me.

JOHN

Yes but.

But

I'm here.

. . .

(*Referring to attractiveness*) And also you're . . .
I mean in terms of
"things you've got going for you."
You're also . . .

                    JESS
What.

                    JOHN
Cmon.

                    JESS
What.

                    JOHN
You know.

                    JESS
No, what.

. . .

                    JOHN
Can you um
can you fix my—

                    JESS
Yeah.

(*She adjusts his clothes. She is close to him.*)

                    JOHN
You um . . .

JESS

Yeah?

JOHN

You smell good.

(Jess and John feel how close they are to each other.)

JESS

Perfume.
Samples.

I take em from magazines.

JOHN

It's nice.

JESS

It's prob'ly yer soap. On me.

(Jess moves away to return to work.)

So how did you judge // me——?

JOHN

Your body.

(This catches Jess.)

For one.

(Was that a compliment? Flirtation?)

Whether you can
lift me.

. . .

JESS

Okay.
And?

JOHN

And how you
move.

JESS

And how's that?

JOHN

Why don't you go out?

JESS

Much

JOHN

At all. Why
not? Someone like you?

. . .

JESS

(A dare; she knows what he means) Someone like what, John.

JOHN

(Knows she knows what he means) And because you went to school
here. Was another way I
judged you.
It means you're not a dumbass.

JESS

Yer not gonna say it?

JOHN

Fuck nope, Jess.
Quite right.
Fuck nope.

(Jess should have finished dressing John by now. She takes in her work.)

How do I look?

JESS

Good.

JOHN

Good.

. . .

Good.

JESS

(Preparing to leave, putting on a winter coat) Okay, well if—

JOHN

Are you around tonight?

JESS

Am I, around?

JOHN

This— . . . ?

JESS

Friday night?

JOHN

Would you
want to come over?

JESS

"Come over?"

JOHN

At seven?

JESS

You don't usually ask me to come by at night.

JOHN

I know.

JESS

And on a Friday night.

JOHN

I know it's late //notice—

JESS

(Finality) Yes. Yeah. I would. I wanna come over. Tonight.

. . .

JOHN   JESS

Yeah?   Wait.

JESS

Lemme um, lemme just call 'n' see if I can—

JOHN

Right.
No of course. // Right.

JESS

No y'know what Fuck it.

JOHN

No, don't // do that.

JESS

Someone'll cover. I'm sure. Fuck it. Yes.

(She's convincing no one.)

JOHN

Are you // sure?

JESS

(Rapid-fire) It's just—Friday night, I make the most on—and they're hard to, y'know, cuz you gotta work *up* to— They start you on Mondays Tuesdays shit days til you— Fridays are— And they don't always give em back if— Which is fucked— And there won't be as much—cuz, December now— And Fridays are—no yeah—yeah no— But everyone wants— But no yeah no someone'll want that. Someone'll take that. Someone'll jump on a Friday shift.
I'll see you at seven.

JOHN

. . . Are you // sure?

JESS

Yes.

JOHN

Yeah?

. . .

JESS

Yeah.
Love to.
I'd love to come over. Tonight.

Yes.

                    JOHN
Good.

                    JESS
Good.

                    JOHN
Cool.

*(She wipes some saliva that has collected on his mouth,
perhaps with a little extra care and sensuality.)*

                    JESS
Cool.

                    JOHN
Tonight.

                    JESS
Yeah okay.

(She looks at him. A spark in her.)

Tonight.

*(And she exits the bathroom.
With some sass in her step.)*

Six

October. Ani's apartment.
Ani is being sponged in a bath by Eddie.

A radio on.
It plays quietly in the background.

We watch them a while.

ANI

I fuckin hate this.

EDDIE

I know you do.

ANI

Cuz it woulda been good to feel this before. To have had you do
this kinda stuff with me before.

It's nice.

You fuckin prick.

(A moment of washing.)

You coulda done this when it // mattered—

EDDIE

How's the water?

ANI

Good.
I'm tired of yellin at you.

EDDIE

Me too. Of you yellin at me.

ANI

I've thrown every awful string a words I could think of at you
these past few days 'n' I'm a very creative // person but yer still
here.

EDDIE

That's true you had some good lines.

ANI

You come back.
I thought you'da gone but yer here.
I don't trust that. There's something about that I don't trust.

EDDIE

Say the word 'n' I'll go.

. . .

ANI

Yeah I don't trust that. You'll be back.

(A moment of washing.)

How's the water feel?

EDDIE

Hm?

ANI

To you?, how's it feel?

EDDIE

Oh shit is it too cold? Shit sorry. // Sorry sorry.

ANI

No no no. It's good for me.
I'm askin fer you. How's it feel to you?
Yer hands are in it too.
I just don't want it to be too cold fer you either. Also.
I also want it to be nice fer you.

You prick.

EDDIE

That's nice of you.

ANI

It is, prick. I know.

EDDIE

(Referring to the water) It's great.
Thank you.
It's great fer me.

*(His hands reach into the tub.
Between her legs.*

*They stay there a minute. Frozen.
Or pull away.)*

. . .

ANI

You *can*.

EDDIE

What?

(A look.)

Oh.
Oh.

ANI

You may have um
noticed
when you were—

EDDIE

// Uh-huh.

ANI

undressing me // that—

EDDIE

Yeah.

*(She pauses for Eddie to get it.
Eddie is getting something completely different.)*

I don't think I should, Ani. It might complicate // things—

ANI

No so I started bleeding, it's my— // —this morning—

EDDIE

Oh!
Right.

ANI

See this is why I wanted a lady to do this.

EDDIE

No no I can, it's not // weird. I can—

ANI

I'm not askin you to . . . inside, I'm—jesus— It's not any sorta
wild—action that I'd need ya to do here. I just I know you usually avoid that area. In general. Lately. *(Sudden embarrassment)*
jesus christ.

EDDIE

It's fine.

ANI

Just since yer cleaning, // y'know, *around* that area—

EDDIE

It's okay.
It's fine it's fine.

. . .

It's fine.

Like this?

. . .
. . .

ANI

Yeah.

EDDIE

It's fine.

. . .

ANI

I can't feel much.
Of anything. There.
I just want you to know in case yer like . . . feelin weird.

EDDIE

I'm not.
I don't feel weird.
Totally normal.

ANI

I'm not sayin I don't. Or I won't. I could.

I feel that . . . kind of feeling.

It's just not on that part of my body.

. . .

EDDIE

Where is it?

. . .

ANI

It's somewhere else.

. . .

(The sound of hands in water.)

. . .

I imagine things.
It's all imagining now. I imagine things.

EDDIE

What things?

ANI

Nice things.

In case you were wondering.

That's what I do these days.
My mind is a great lover.

(Ani rethinks.)

It's a good lover.

It's my memory I worry about. My mind's limited. I can only really imagine . . . variations of what already happened in my life. But in like, slightly different ways. So my imagination's got all this . . . grime that won't come off it from my memories.

*(Eddie's hands in the water
are doing something to Ani
that she has loved for years.
We should not know this has been happening until we hear how he talks
to her.)*

EDDIE

You can't feel this?

What I'm doin right now?

. . .

You can't feel that?

. . .
. . .
. . .

ANI

No.

(Eddie stops.
And he continues washing.

A song of slow piano from the radio.*)

EDDIE

You listenin to this song?

ANI

Hm?, what?
Yeah.
Yeah it's nice don't change it.

EDDIE

You wanna learn to play it?

ANI

Hilarious.

———————

* We used Erik Satie's *Gnossienne No. 1* as played by Reinbert de Leeuw.

EDDIE

No I mean I can't play it either. Not like, traditionally.
Always wanted to learn though. Anything. Any kinda instrument.
The sax. // Or, y'know, or maybe the piano.

ANI

God, not the fuckin *sax*. Oh yeah piano, okay.

EDDIE

Think it woulda been cool to learn.

ANI

Well.
You still could.

EDDIE

Used to pretend I could. My folks, they got me this little keyboard
for Christmas once. Li'l Casio. They thought I'd be a champ at it.
Long fingers, y'know. And I wanted to learn Tried but. Nothing.
And it killed me cuz I mean they *bought* it—with money they
ain't really have, y'know. They bought it without realizin how
much lessons cost and that school don't give em.
So I'd pretend to be able to play.
There was this control on it where you could still play it but no
sound had to come out. So I'd imagine what it'd sound like. To
play. If I could.
I'd put the radio on. Find the station where they play piano. And
I'd act like I was playin that.
Beautiful stuff. I'd act like that was me playin that.

. . .

(Referring to the radio) It's a good song.

ANI

You never told me.

EDDIE

Hm?

ANI

You never told me that.

(They listen.

Then:

Eddie takes one of Ani's arms,
and drapes it along the bathtub edge.)

What're you doin?

(Eddie rests one hand on her arm,
then the other
and he begins to "play" Ani's arms like a piano.

He mimes the music that's playing on the radio.

It should look like the music is coming from Ani's body.

He's good.
He knows the song.
His fingers are beautifully accurate with the piano music.

It lasts long enough to move something in the two.)

EDDIE

Always wish I could.

(He plays.)

You feel that?

. . .

. . .

. . .

ANI

Yeah.

. . .

(He stops playing. Returns her arm to the water.)

. . .

EDDIE

What do you wanna do fer yer birthday?
Weather's supposed to be nice next month.

ANI

It'll be November. In New Jersey.
And you can't tell weather that far in advance.

EDDIE

We can plan on it bein nice. 'N' if it's not, then we'll roll with it.

ANI

"We"?

EDDIE

What would you wanna do?

ANI

You won't be here.

EDDIE

Why not?

ANI

You got yer drive.

EDDIE

What if I took off?

ANI

'N' what if you paid yer bills?
Don't take off work.

EDDIE

Listen woman I'm gonna do what I'm gonna do.

ANI

(Not unkindly) Don't promise me things, Eddie.

. . .

EDDIE

What would you wanna do?

(Ani looks at him suspiciously.)

ANI

Mm. You wouldn't like it.

EDDIE

It's not about me.

ANI

Maine.
I wanna go to Maine.
Fer my birthday.

. . .

. . .

EDDIE

It's cold up there / / right?

ANI

See?

EDDIE

And it rains a lot and it's all like, fancy boats 'n' shit? / / Lobsters.

ANI

Yer thinkin of Seattle.

EDDIE

They got fancy boats there too, right?

ANI

Maybe. Never been. That's why I wanna go.

EDDIE

Okay yeah but Maine? That's like—Canada. Why you wanna go to Maine?

ANI

I saw this picture once on Janey's desk—some trip she took with her kids after the divorce. To Maine. / / The—

EDDIE

Like, a photo? You wanna go to Canada cuz of a—? Shit, I'll show you some photos of Cancún, you'll change yer mind about, fuckin, Canada.

ANI

The frame was made outta wood but like, real wood. It was just
four little twigs tied together but somehow it looked nicer than
if someone tried to fix it into wood. And Janey's got a hat on—
cuz it's so *sunny* in Maine—so you can't see her eyes but you can
see her mouth which looked . . . It's her in a field and she's holdin
a stick like a cane. It's just her . . . by herself . . . and she's . . . fine.
And there's a lot of green.

EDDIE

Is that . . . ? Is that where you were goin? That night?

ANI

That's what they told me later. When the ambulance found me,
they said that's what I said.
I wasn't. But.
But maybe I would've. If I'd kept drivin.

I'd hafta change a bunch of doctor's appointments if I went anywhere fer my birthday.

EDDIE

Yeah but. Yer birthday!

ANI

Yeah but I don't wanna fuck around. With appointments.
And it costs a lot to . . . do anything. Fer me to do anything.

Don't take off work.

EDDIE

I tore up the papers.

ANI

What?

EDDIE

Or I will.
I will. When I get home.
The divorce papers.

ANI

Don't talk about papers right now.

EDDIE

Okay.

ANI

Papers were trees.

(A moment of not talking.)

EDDIE

Can you smoke in here?

ANI

I can do anything I want in here.

(Eddie lights a cigarette.
He alternates puffs between them, using his hands.
One for him. One for her. For him. For her.
They don't need language for this.
He knows she'd want some.

The following is quiet and simple.
They know each other better than anyone.)

She leave you?

EDDIE

What?

ANI

Did she leave you?

EDDIE

No.

Not yet.

But the . . . clouds are there.

ANI

People are hard.

(They smoke.)

What are you gonna do?

. . .

. . .

EDDIE

Is there a world, Ani, where . . . where you and—?

ANI

No.

. . .

. . .

*(We should think he understands. And drops it.
But—)*

EDDIE

Why not?

ANI

(Not antagonistically, just clear-eyed) If I give you reasons, Eddie, you'll just—talk. It's not a game where you gather up all yer points fer this 'n' pit em against all my points fer that 'n' who's right 'n' who's wrong. It's not like that anymore. If you wanna help me, you can help me. You helped me.

But if you ever came back . . . like, Came Back . . . I'd need to know it was fer me. Not fer . . . anything else.

(A rare glimpse into her longing) If I weren't like this right now, would you be here?

. . .

EDDIE

Yeah.
Yes.

. . .

ANI

That's not a thing I'll ever know.
Everything's started over fer me—

EDDIE

It doesn't have to though.

ANI

If everything was perfect in yer life, no holes you had to fill, you wouldn't be here.

EDDIE

That's not how people work. People don't go after people *unless* they fuckin need em. And everyone fuckin—needs em, someone. That's what life is, what yer life, my life . . . is. Okay? That's how people work. In life.

Where's yer ashtray?

ANI

They prob'ly didn't pack it. Fer fuckin, my own fuckin good 'n'
shit, the fucks.
Check the kitchen though.

EDDIE

Be back. Don't go anywhere.

(Eddie gets up to exit the bathroom.)

ANI

Hey.

(He stops.)

EDDIE

What's up?

ANI

It's been nice to get to know you.
Again.
This week.

EDDIE

You too.

ANI

You prick.

EDDIE

Maybe you'll take me to Maine one day.

ANI

Yeah.

Maybe.

Maybe I'll see you there one day.

EDDIE

Or you'll take me. I wiped yer fuckin ass this week—

ANI

Oh my // God.

EDDIE

Fer *free.* You owe me fuckin—Canada.

ANI

Go to the fuckin kitchen.

(He smiles at her.
She smiles at him.
The pricks.)

EDDIE

Be back.

(Eddie leaves the room.

Ani alone.
She sits with herself in the tub.)

ANI

(To Eddie offstage) I think I'm gonna go back to work. In a few months. See Janey. Everyone. What do you think? Think I'll do that. I'd like to.

(She awaits a response.)

Eddie?

(He can't hear her.

She stares out. Sits with herself in the tub.
She starts to wonder where he is.
Tries to turn her head.)

Eddie? Did you hear—

(Suddenly, she slips down into the tub.
Not intentional.
Becomes submerged.

We hear yelling from under water.

From off, we hear rummaging in the kitchen.

Eventually, Eddie returns, holding a plate for an ashtray.
He drops the plate and reaches into the tub
to retrieve Ani. She gasps for air.

He holds her against him.

She gasps.)

You can't leave me in the—
You can't leave me in—

EDDIE

I'm sorry.

ANI

You can't—
You can't—
You—

EDDIE

I'm sorry.

(She gasps.)

ANI

Don't go.

(He holds her to him.)

Seven

Friday evening.
John's apartment.

Nice lighting.
Music plays.

Jess enters. She carries a black plastic shopping bag. Sets it down.
She shakes snow off of her. Takes off her coat.
She's dressed up. Lookin good. Feelin good.
She takes in the music and mood-lighting. Impressive.

She adjusts her dress. Tights. Hair.
Pulls a magazine sample of perfume from her bag
and applies it to her chest and maybe under her arms.
She looks back to see if he might be coming,
and then she also applies some between her thighs.

She poses, ready.

JESS

John?

(Flush, offstage.)

JOHN

(From off) You're
early.

*(John enters.
He turns off the music with a remote.)*

You're dressed so—

JESS

Yeah.

JOHN

Nice.

JESS

It's true.

JOHN

You look nice.

JESS

Well, you only see me in the mornings so—

JOHN

I need a shower, though, and // you're all—

JESS

Oh. A—?
(Intrigued) Yeah?
Yeah okay.

JOHN

Could we maybe
start with a shower?

JESS

I can get into that.

JOHN

I know this is a bit
different
from our usual—

JESS

Uh-huh.

JOHN

And then maybe a shave.
An extra good shave.

JESS

I can do that.

JOHN

I thought if it was too early, like
early in the week or this morning, if you shaved me too early,
I'd be prickly.

JESS

Cuz yer a fuckin gentleman like that.

JOHN

And you're
good at it.
And . . .

JESS

Uh-huh . . .

JOHN

And I'm nervous.

JESS

You don't hafta be nervous.

JOHN

And excited!

JESS

Well it's good to talk before.

JOHN

I used to consider hookers.

JESS

Yeah but maybe let's not talk about that.

JOHN

Yes that's not a very manly conversation. I used to think when
I spoke of
hookers it would be manly.

JESS

Don't talk about hookers.

JOHN

But I just wouldn't know where to start
looking for—see, another unmanly, I simply shouldn't ever talk
about hookers.

JESS

No.

JOHN

But if we don't talk about how far we've come, Jess, not
doing certain things, how will anyone know how
far we've come?

JESS

What do you wanna do first?

JOHN

Brag.

JESS

Well how bout I could shave you first.

JOHN

Good plan.

JESS

Then shower.

JOHN

Yes.

JESS

So the cream, the—

JOHN

Right. I see where you're going with that.

JESS

—the shaving cream would get washed right off yer body. In the shower.

JOHN

Do we have time for both?

JESS

Fuck yes.

JOHN

I'm meeting her at eight.

. . .

JESS

Wait.

JOHN

(In his own world) Mm. What time is Maybe I should skip one. If I had to skip one, shower or shave: which?

JESS

For a . . .

JOHN

First date!

JESS

With a . . .

JESS	JOHN
Hooker?	Graduate student!

JOHN

Madelyn.
From *Oxford*.
From *actual* Oxford.
PhD with a focus in *Hume*,
the minx.
I'm meeting her at eight. Just like her figure.
How does one even do this.
When someone's so—*[wonderful]*
There's just something so
[wonderful]
about her.

*(Amid this, while John is oblivious,
Jess takes from her plastic bag a bottle of wine.
Opens it. A twist off. Pours a glass.)*

What is this?

JESS

Pinot.

(She puts a straw in his glass.)

JOHN

Good idea.

(He drinks from the straw. And wonders.)

Oh Jess.
Jess Jess.
How does one do it?

(She drinks from the bottle.)

JESS

(As if to herself) Shave and a shower.

JOHN

Shave and a shower, yes.
Please.
Thank you.

JESS

What time you gonna be done?

JOHN

What?

JESS

With yer date.

JOHN

Well that
depends. *Late*, I hope.
Oh, but you don't have to wait up.
You can go after this. And I can
pay you for the whole—

JESS

But like two hours? Four? Dinner and a movie? Four hours? Five?

JOHN

Oh. I'm not // sure—

JESS

Could I stay here?

. . .

JOHN

In my
apartment?

JESS

Just while yer gone.
I'd like to stay here.

JOHN

. . . Why?

JESS

I won't fuck with yer shit. Promise.

JOHN

But . . . without me here?

JESS

I just want one night.
I just want something that's mine fer one night.
Even if it's yours.

Say yes.

JOHN

But—

JESS

Because I took off work.
On the night I make most my money fer the week. To live.
So I could be here.
With you.

(John sees her dress.
The wine.

Her face.)

JOHN

Oh.

JESS

No one's gonna be here, right? This place will just be here. Warm 'n' empty. With no one in it while yer gone.

JOHN

Yeah but—

JESS

Say yes.

JOHN

. . .

JESS

. . .

JOHN

I don't really . . .
I
I'm sorry but
I don't
feel comfortable. You here.
Without me.

JESS

Why.

JOHN

I just—

JESS

Why.

JOHN

You've taken some
stuff // before—

JESS

What stuff.

JOHN

It doesn't—

JESS

What.

JOHN

Soap.

I know you took, which— It's fine.
It's just*[soap]*— But—
I would rather be here.
Whenever you are.

That's all.

JESS

I can give it back.

JOHN

It's fine.

. . .

Why'd you take it?

. . .

JESS

I can give it back.

JOHN

Could we just
Let's just
Shave and a shower.

And I'll pay you overtime,
since you're over time.

Okay?

JESS

Shave and a shower.
Okay.
Yeah.

JOHN

Thanks.

*(An awkwardness and strangeness hangs between them.
Something's changed for good.)*

Hey at least you'll get to
go home early.
For a change.

JESS

Right.

(John exits toward the bathroom.)

. . .

(Jess stands a moment . . .)

Right.

(. . . then runs out of the apartment, her coat in her arms.)

Eight

Jess has just run out of John's apartment, humiliated and lost.
It snows around her.
She takes out her cell and makes a call.

The disappointment of an answering machine.
Raw need floods a non-English language.

JESS
(Italics not in parenthesis indicate words spoken in another language)
I was really hoping you'd pick up. *I miss you so much. I wish I could
talk to you. (Referring to illness) I wish you were——still you.*
I love you.
I'm sorry. I just——I miss you. I'm sorry. I'm sorry.
I'm sorry.

Bye, *Mommy.*

(She hangs up.

She looks up and watches the snow falling from the sky.

Snow.
Wind.
Night.

Jess exits.)

Nine, or Epilogue

Eddie's apartment.
Boxes inside. Snow outside.
Later that night.
Something feels different.

Eddie enters, goes to a box. Rummages through it.

EDDIE
(To someone offstage) It's somewhere in here sorry. Sorry I know it's in here somewhere.

(He rummages.)

You wanna come in? Warm up a bit while I—

(He rummages. Sees this person has not budged.)

Or—okay. Or keep enjoyin the view.
Of Bayonne.

(Jess walks into the door frame, careful, alert, suspicious. And on the defensive.
She wears a coat. Beneath it, the dress she wore to John's, over the warm-est sweatpants and winter boots she owns. She does not fully enter yet.)

You can see pretty much the whole rest of the apartment from where yer standin. So that's the tour.
But you can also come in.
If you want.

JESS

Where is she?

EDDIE

Oh.
She kinda comes 'n' goes—

JESS

Yer wife kinda comes 'n' goes?

EDDIE

We're uh—
We're separating so she—

JESS

You said you 'n' yer wife live here. That's why // I was even will-ing to come near here.

EDDIE

We do. We did.

JESS

So where is she? She gonna be hidin in the closet? In one a these boxes? Somebody gonna jump out these boxes and like, take my organs— *(Referring to the door)* Keep it open.

You really got a wife?

(He shows her a picture from his wallet.)

Could be yer sister.

EDDIE

It's not.
And anyway, even if it was, wouldn't it calm you down you just met a dude carries around pictures of his—adopted—sister?

JESS

Just sayin, not really a lady's touch in here.

EDDIE

Well neither is that car you were sleepin in. Miss Lady.

You checkin to see if I had money?

JESS

What?

EDDIE

In my wallet.

JESS

No. What? // No, man—

EDDIE

See, this is why people don't help people.

JESS

(Turning to exit) This was a stupid idea—

EDDIE

Just drink some tea at least!
If yer just gonna go back 'n' fuckin, sleep in yer car all night—then
come in a minute, have some tea.

(She stops. Snow falls around her in the door frame.)

It's awful outside. And you, out there, in yer icebox of a car.
I woulda invited you in no matter who you were. A man or a—

JESS

Right.

EDDIE

I woulda.
One A.M. on a Friday night, you don't know who could be out
there.

JESS

I've been doin this a few weeks now, I can handle myself.

EDDIE

A few weeks?, you been sleepin in yer—?

JESS

I usually have heat goin. But the battery died.
Where's the—

EDDIE

Found it.

(He finds a blanket in one of the boxes. Ani's blanket.
He hesitates
then hands it to Jess.)

JESS

Thank you. This is really gonna be—Thanks—helpful. Out there.

(She is about to leave—)

EDDIE

If you could just—leave it by the door? In the morning? Or whenever yer done // with—

JESS

Yeah, okay.

EDDIE

Appreciate it.

Sentimental.

(Jess is about to leave—
then remembers where she's come from and where she's going. Pauses.)

JESS

I'm just gonna warm up for a minute.

EDDIE

Okay.

JESS

That's all.
Then I'm gone.

. . .

EDDIE

I got pizza should still be good. I can heat it.
(Carefully) I won't . . . I won't give you money. But I'll feed you.

I knew a lady, not far from here, she died in her car doin what yer doin. She'd keep her car runnin while she was sleepin in it and a gas can in the back in case she ran outta— And one night it tipped over. A lady. Young. Thirty-two or something, thirty-three. They found her in the morning. Suffocated. The fumes. A stupid thing. Small, stupid things.
A gas can.
And then she—wasn't.

I saw you in yer car and I—I dunno, you never know, y'know?

(Jess hasn't moved.
Snow around her.)

I got pizza. If you want it.

JESS

What kind?

EDDIE

Plain.

JESS

It's good?

EDDIE

From last night.

You gonna come in?

. . .

JESS

I dunno get the pizza.

. . .

EDDIE

You gonna steal my shit? While I heat this slice?

JESS

What shit am I gonna steal? 'N' put where?

. . .

. . .

EDDIE

Don't steal my shit.

(*Eddie exits to heat a slice. We hear a microwave in the darkness of the apartment.*

Jess stands—looking around—but always near the door.

Eddie returns. The microwave hums in the distance.)

JESS

I work.

EDDIE

Okay.

JESS

I'm not some kinda—just sleepin in a car, okay? // I work.

EDDIE

Okay.

JESS

Til four A.M. some nights.
At bars, so don't get any ideas.
I woulda usually been workin tonight. Fer most of the night.
I—I wasn't tonight. But I usually woulda.

(The microwave beeps.)

I'm not some fuckin—just sleeps in a car. I went to school. I work.

EDDIE

You wanna come inside?

JESS

I am inside.

EDDIE

More inside?

JESS

I'm good here.

EDDIE

Okay but the snow is—

JESS

Oh.

EDDIE

I mean, I don't have any nice stuff or anything, *rugs*, that I'm like,
worried about here but—snow's fallin inside.
I don't want you to trip.

JESS

I'm careful.

EDDIE

Okay.

*(She still stands by the door.
Then,*

she takes one step closer in.
And closes the door slightly—still keeping it open. Ready.)

Want me to take yer // coat?

JESS

I don't walk into houses, I want you to know that, I also don't just walk into houses.

EDDIE

Yeah of course—

JESS

I'm careful. I sleep during the day—usually—cuz I'm so careful. I arranged my life so I work at night—til // four A.M. some nights—

EDDIE

Til four A.M. yeah that's late.

JESS

Don't make fuckin fun of me, you ever work all fuckin night?

EDDIE

Yeah. Yes. I have.
Lots of times actually.
Too many.

JESS

. . . Okay.
Okay so you know.
I sleep at different points in the day, at some point in the day. People leave me alone, mostly. They see someone asleep in their car but it's in the day, the early day, and they kinda leave you alone. Mostly.

EDDIE

It's cold though.

JESS

Yeah.
Yeah I haven't figured that all out yet. This season.
It is.
It's cold.

(*She sees the past few months of her life in her mind. Tries to pretend they aren't there.*)

It's really fuckin cold.

(*The microwave beeps again. A reminder.*)

It's little breaks, y'know? Car. The car. Health stuff, some prob- lems—that cleans you out fast. Bad luck. Mistakes. Some mistakes. Was hoppin on couches fer a while but that gets old quick—bein the one that always needs something. I got old.

EDDIE

Where's yer . . . ?

JESS

I don't have family here, not anymore, in the country.
She got sick 'n' went back.
We couldn't afford—not here.
I've been sendin money but it's—you know—

EDDIE

Yeah.

JESS	EDDIE
Not enough.	Never enough.

JESS

So I'm sleepin in her car.
I can send more that way.

We used to live not far from here. So that's where I park.

EDDIE

By my place.

JESS

Yeah.

EDDIE

So we're neighbors.

. . .

She died.

JESS

Yeah I know, the woman in the car—

EDDIE

No. My wife. She died. Last month.
Please don't go.
Or you can go. If you want. But don't. Please.
We can have an arrangement. You can crash every once in a while.
Or
Or you can live here.
We can split the place. This place. I'll pay more. I don't have much,
y'know, money but. I'm outta work now but I'll get employed
again. I just—I need someone here. I just need someone here.
With me.
I'm sorry yer a woman.
Not *that* yer a woman but I know that makes this all a little weird.

I keep the lights on now. Every room. All the time.
I would pay fer those! You wouldn't hafta pay fer those.
It's . . . it's just um . . . being alone . . . here is . . .
I don't know what to do—

(The microwave beeps.)

JESS

The pizza's . . .

EDDIE

Yeah.
Yeah okay.

(This feels to Eddie like a defeat.
But he will still get the slices. Eddie exits.

Jess looks around.
She closes the door.
It's instantly warmer.

Jess considers.

Eddie returns with two slices of pizza on paper towels.)

(Referring to the paper towels) Plates were dirty. Didn't wanna make
you wait.

(She sees him. Sees something in him.

He sees something too.
In this moment, he doesn't think he'll ever see this person again.)

You want it, um, To-Go? In a bag?

JESS

How much is rent?

EDDIE

Twelve! We can prorate it!

JESS

Don't get too excited.

EDDIE

(He is) I'm not!

JESS

Yer not excited I could be livin with you?

EDDIE

I am. I // "would."

JESS

Don't get excited. I'm just askin.

EDDIE

I'm not a weird person either.

JESS

Cool I trust you now.

EDDIE

I don't even go to bars. Not usually. Or stay out late.

JESS

But you were tonight.

EDDIE

But I'm usually not. I'm usually not so I wouldn't have usually even seen you out there, that late, in yer car. This was an unusual thing I did tonight. I was goin to meet someone.
I got stood up actually.
By a—

I was on my way home. And I found you.

JESS

Oh you didn't "find" me.

EDDIE

Okay.

JESS

You saw me.
I *let* you see me.

I was just askin. About the rent. Just——to ask.

EDDIE

Sit. Eat.

JESS

I'll stand.

EDDIE

Okay.

(*He holds out her slice.*)

JESS

Take a bite of my pizza.

(He does.
Ta-da. Still alive.
Then he gives her the slice.
She holds it, unsure whether to eat it.
Or to stay.)

EDDIE

The poison's gonna take at least an hour so we got some time still to conversate.

(She stares at him.
He laughs.
He laughs at his own joke.
Maybe he laughs too loud and too long.
Maybe he becomes devastated at thinking about death,
even joking about it, at this moment in his life.
Maybe he thought he was okay sooner than he really is.

Something happens to a very lonely man here.)

I'm not a weird person.

JESS

I think I'm gonna go.

EDDIE

Do you have tea? Fer the car?

JESS

I don't have any way to make hot water.

EDDIE

I'll give you some. Please don't go.

(She puts down the slice somewhere.)

149

Take the slice.

JESS

That's okay.

EDDIE

What's yer name?

JESS

(Exiting) I'm sorry.

EDDIE

What's yer number?

JESS

No.

EDDIE

(Approaching her) Area code? Did you get a new number recently? What's yer area code?

JESS

I have mace in my bag!

(He freezes. Hands up.)

EDDIE

. . . Thank you fer tellin me. Instead of just—

JESS

You don't seem like—
It's just unfortunate that some people have already lived a lot of life before they meet other people.
I'm sorry.

(Jess goes to the door.)

EDDIE

Just—okay—be careful though, okay?
Stupid things. It can be a small, stupid thing. A blood clot while
I was gone on a drive. A tiny vein. And then she wasn't.

JESS

(About your wife) I'm sorry.
(About leaving) But . . . I'm sorry.

EDDIE

Just—be careful.
And—and make sure someone's watchin you, I guess, in
y'know . . . in some kinda way.

JESS

973.

EDDIE

What?

JESS

Is my area code. 973.

. . .

EDDIE

Oh.
Okay.
(Disappointed) She was 201.

JESS

Thanks fer . . . trying.

EDDIE

Thanks fer . . . yeah . . . you too.

(Jess exits.

Eddie takes off his coat.
It slumps or hangs somewhere.

He stands alone in his space a moment.

He goes to the pizza she left.
And he holds it in his hands.
. . .

Then,
Eddie's phone buzzes
from somewhere within his coat.

He stops.
He turns toward it.

Stands.

. . .

He fears going to his phone.

. . .

Then,
the doorknob turns.
He jumps back.

Snow.
Wind.)

Come in.

(Snow.

Then,
Jess enters.

She has a thermos with her.
She stands with the snow around her.)

JESS

I brought coffee. But it's old.

EDDIE

I have pizza.
But
it's cold.

You wanna come in?

(She takes off her hat.
And takes one step inside.
Toward Eddie.

He takes one step toward her.

Two people stand together in a fading light.)

END OF PLAY

MARTYNA MAJOK was born in Bytom, Poland, and raised in New Jersey and Chicago. She was awarded the 2018 Pulitzer Prize for Drama for *Cost of Living* (Williamstown Theatre Festival, Manhattan Theatre Club). Other plays include *Sanctuary City* (New York Theatre Workshop), *Queens* (LCT3/Lincoln Center, La Jolla Playhouse), and *Ironbound* (Steppenwolf Theatre Company, Round House Theatre, WP Theater/Rattlestick Playwrights Theater, Geffen Playhouse, and other theaters in America and abroad). Majok's awards include The Lucille Lortel Award for Outstanding Play, The Greenfield Prize (first female recipient in drama), Francesca Primus Prize, two Jane Chambers Playwriting Awards, The Lanford Wilson Prize, The Lilly Award's Stacey Mindich Prize, the Helen Merrill Emerging Playwright Award, the Charles MacArthur Award for Outstanding New Play from the Helen Hayes Awards, Jean Kennedy Smith Playwriting Award, the ANPF Women's Invitational Prize, the David Calicchio Emerging American Playwright Prize, the Global Age Project Prize, an NYTW 2050 Fellowship, the NNPN Smith Prize for Political Playwriting, and The Merage Foundation Fellowship for the American Dream. She received an MFA from the Yale School of Drama and Juilliard, and a BA from the University of Chicago. She is an alumna of the Ensemble Studio Theatre's Youngblood and WP Lab. She is a Core Writer at the Playwrights' Center, an NYTW Usual Suspect, and a member of the Dramatists Guild and the Writers Guild of America East. Majok was the 2015–2016 PoNY Fellow at the Lark Play Development Center and is a 2018–2019 Hodder Fellow at Princeton University.

Theatre Communications Group would like to offer our special thanks to the Vilcek Foundation for its generous support of the publication of Cost of Living *by Martyna Majok*

THE VILCEK FOUNDATION raises awareness of immigrant contributions in America and fosters appreciation of the arts and sciences. Established in 2000 by Jan and Marica Vilcek, immigrants from the former Czechoslovakia, the Foundation's mission was inspired by the couple's respective careers in biomedical science and art history, as well as their appreciation for the opportunities offered to them as newcomers to the United States.

TCG books sponsored by the Vilcek Foundation include:

Mr. Burns and Other Plays by Anne Washburn
Cost of Living by Martyna Majok
The Detroit Project by Dominique Morisseau
Five Plays by Sam Hunter

THEATRE COMMUNICATIONS GROUP (TCG), the national organization for the American theatre, promotes the idea of "A Better World for Theatre, and a Better World Because of Theatre." In addition to TCG's numerous services to the theatre field, TCG Books is the nation's largest independent publisher of dramatic literature, with 16 Pulitzer Prizes for Drama on its book list. The book program commits to the life-long career of its playwrights, keeping all of their plays in print. TCG Books' other authors include: Annie Baker, Nilo Cruz, Quiara Alegría Hudes, David Henry Hwang, Tony Kushner, Donald Margulies, Suzan-Lori Parks, Sarah Ruhl, Stephen Sondheim, Anne Washburn, and August Wilson, among many others.

Support TCG's work in the theatre field by becoming a member or donor: www.tcg.org

tcg